# CAKES & CANDIES

## Colour By Number

Book by Sachin Sachdeva (Author/Illustrator)

1= Yellow 2=Blue 3= Green 4=Pink
5=Purple 6=Orange 7=Red 8=Brown

1= Yellow    2=Blue    3= Green    4=Pink

5=Purple    6=Orange    7=Red    8=Brown

1= Yellow    2=Blue    3= Green    4=Pink
5=Purple    6=Orange    7=Red    8=Brown

1= Yellow     2=Blue     3= Green     4=Pink

5=Purple     6=Orange     7=Red     8=Brown

1= Yellow    2=Blue    3= Green    4=Pink

5=Purple    6=Orange    7=Red    8=Brown

1= Yellow　　2=Blue　　3= Green　　4=Pink

5=Purple　　6=Orange　　7=Red　　8=Brown

1= Yellow      2=Blue      3= Green      4=Pink

5=Purple      6=Orange      7=Red      8=Brown

1= Yellow    2=Blue    3= Green    4=Pink

5=Purple    6=Orange    7=Red    8=Brown

1= Yellow    2=Blue    3= Green    4=Pink

5=Purple    6=Orange    7=Red    8=Brown

1= Yellow     2=Blue     3= Green     4=Pink

5=Purple     6=Orange     7=Red     8=Brown

1= Yellow    2=Blue    3= Green    4=Pink
5=Purple    6=Orange    7=Red    8=Brown

1= Yellow     2=Blue     3= Green     4=Pink

5=Purple     6=Orange     7=Red     8=Brown

1= Yellow        2=Blue        3= Green        4=Pink

5=Purple        6=Orange        7=Red        8=Brown

1= Yellow    2=Blue    3= Green    4=Pink

5=Purple    6=Orange    7=Red    8=Brown

1= Yellow        2=Blue        3= Green        4=Pink
5=Purple        6=Orange        7=Red        8=Brown

1= Yellow          2=Blue          3= Green          4=Pink

5=Purple          6=Orange          7=Red          8=Brown

1= Yellow     2=Blue     3= Green     4=Pink

5=Purple     6=Orange     7=Red     8=Brown

1= Yellow        2=Blue        3= Green        4=Pink

5=Purple        6=Orange        7=Red        8=Brown

1= Yellow     2=Blue     3= Green     4=Pink

5=Purple     6=Orange     7=Red     8=Brown

I hope your child like the book and learned coloring the pages. I will appreciate if you could take a minute from your busy schedule and leave a feedback.
It really helps :-)

Thank you
Sachin Sachdeva (Author & Illustrator)
www.inkytreasure.com

You can give your feedback and suggestions on Amazon.com

Made in the USA
Middletown, DE
03 December 2019